Primary Geography

Teacher's Book 6 Issues

Stephen Scoffham | Colin Bridge

Geography in the primary school   2

Collins Primary Geography   3

Places, themes and skills   4-5

Layout of the units   6-7

Lesson planning   8

Lesson summary   9

Studying the local area   10

Studying places in the UK and wider world   11

Differentiation and progression   12

Assessment   13

High quality geography   14

Ofsted inspections   15

Information on the units   16-25

Copymaster matrix   26-29

Copymasters   30-59

Geography in the English National Curriculum   60-61

Geography in the primary school

Geography is the study of the Earth's surface. It helps children understand the human and physical forces which shape the environment. Children are naturally interested in their immediate surroundings. They also want to know about places beyond their direct experience. Geography is uniquely placed to satisfy this curiosity.

Geographical enquiries

Geography is an enquiry-led subject that seeks to answer fundamental questions such as:

- Where is this place?
- What is this place like (and why)?
- How and why is it changing?
- How does this place compare with other places?
- How and why are places connected?

These questions involve not only finding out about the natural processes which have shaped our environment, they also involve finding out how people have responded to them. Studying this interaction at a range of scales from the local to the global and asking questions about what is happening in the world around us lie at the heart of both academic and school geography.

Geographical perspectives

Geographical perspectives offer a uniquely powerful way of seeing the world. Since the time of the Ancient Greeks geographers have been attempting to chronicle and interpret their surroundings. One way of seeing links and connections is to think in terms of key ideas. Three concepts which geographers have found particularly useful in a range of settings are place, space and scale.

- Place focuses attention on the environment.
- Space focuses attention on location.
- Scale introduces a change in perspective that enables us to link the local and the global.

A layer of secondary concepts such as patterns, change and movement lie beneath these fundamental organising ideas and provide a way of further enhancing our understanding.

As they conduct their enquiries and investigations geographers make use of a number of specific skills. Foremost among these are mapwork and the ability to represent spatial information. The use of maps, charts, diagrams, tables, sketches and other cartographic techniques come under the more general heading of 'graphicacy' and are a distinguishing feature of geographical thinking. As more and more information has come to be represented electronically, the use of computers and other electronic applications has been championed by geography educators.

Geography in primary schools offers children from the earliest ages a fascinating window onto the contemporary world. The challenge for educators is to find ways of providing experiences and selecting content that will help children develop an increasingly deep understanding.

Collins Primary Geography

Collins Primary Geography is a complete programme for pupils in the primary school and can be used as a structure for teaching geography from ages 5-11. It consists of five pupil books and supporting teacher's guides with notes and copymasters. There is one pupil book at Key Stage 1 and four pupil books at Key Stage 2. There is also a supporting DVD for each Key Stage.

Aims

The overall aim of the programme is to inspire children with an enthusiasm for geography and to empower them as learners. The underlying principles include a commitment to international understanding in a more equitable world, a concern for the future welfare of the planet and a recognition that creativity, hope and optimism play a fundamental role in lasting learning. Three different dimensions – connecting to the environment, connecting to each other and connecting to ourselves – are explored throughout the programme in different contexts and at a range of scales. We believe that learning to think geographically in the broadest meaning of the term will help children make wise decisions in the future as they grow into adulthood.

Structure

Collins Primary Geography provides full coverage of the English National Curriculum requirements. Each pupil book covers a balanced range of themes and topics and includes case studies with a more precise focus:

- Book 1 and 2 *World around us* introduces pupils to the world at both a local and global scale.
- Book 3 *Investigation* encourages pupils to conduct their own research and enquiries.
- Book 4 *Movement* considers how movement affects the physical and human environment.
- Book 5 *Change* includes case studies on how places alter and develop.
- Book 6 *Issues* introduces more complex ideas to do with the environment and sustainability.

Although the books are not limited to a specific year band, Book 3 will be particularly suitable for Year 3 children. Similarly, Book 4 is focused on Year 4 children. However it is also possible to trace themes from one book to another. The programme is structured in such a way that key themes are revisited making it possible to investigate a specific topic in greater depth if required.

Investigations

Enquiries and investigations are an important part of pupils' work in primary geography. Asking questions and searching for answers can help children develop key knowledge, understanding and skills. Fieldwork is time consuming when it involves travelling to distant locations, but local area work can be equally effective. Many of the exercises in *Collins Primary Geography* focus on the classroom, school building and local environment. We believe that such activities can have a seminal role in promoting long term positive attitudes towards sustainability and the environment.

Places, themes and skills

Each book is divided into ten units giving a balance between places, themes and skills.

Places

There are locality studies throughout each book and studies of specific places from the UK, Europe and other continents. These studies illustrate how people interact with their physical surroundings in a constantly changing world. The places have been selected so that by the end of the scheme, children will be familiar with a balanced range of reference points from around the world. They should also have developed an increasingly sophisticated locational framework which will enable them to place their new knowledge in context.

Themes

Physical geography is covered in the initial three units of each book which focus on planet Earth, water and weather. Human geography is considered in units on settlements, work and travel. There is also a unit specifically devoted to the urban and rural environment and human impact on the natural world. This is a very important aspect of modern geography and a key topic for schools generally.

Skills

Maps and plans are introduced in context to convey information about the places which are being studied. The books contain maps at scales which range from the local to global and use a range of techniques which children can emulate. Charts, diagrams and other graphical devices are included throughout. Fieldwork is strongly emphasised and all the books include projects and investigations which can be conducted in the local environment.

Information technology

Geography has always been closely associated with information technology. The way in which computers can be used for recording and processing information is illustrated in each of the books. Satellite images are included together with information from data handling packages. Oblique and vertical aerial photographs are included as sources of evidence.

Cross-curricular links

The different units in *Collins Primary Geography* can be easily linked with other subjects. The physical geography units have natural synergies with themes from sciences, as do the units on the environment. Local area studies overlap with work in history. Furthermore, the opportunities for promoting the core subjects are particularly strong. Each lesson is supported by discussion questions and many of the investigations involve written work in different modes and registers.

Places, themes and skills

Places and Themes	Book 3 Units	Book 4 Units	Book 5 Units	Book 6 Units
Planet Earth	Landscapes	Coasts	Seas and oceans	Restless Earth
Water	Water around us	Rivers	Wearing away the land	Drinking water
Weather	Weather worldwide	Weather patterns	The seasons	Local weather
Settlements	Villages	Towns	Cities	Planning issues
Work and travel	Travel	Food and shops	Jobs	Transport
Environment	Caring for the countryside	Caring for towns	Pollution	Conservation
United Kingdom	Scotland	Northern Ireland	Wales	England
Europe	France	Germany	Greece	Europe
North and South America	South America *Chile*	North America *The Rocky Mountains*	North America *Jamaica*	South America *The Amazon*
Asia and Africa	Asia *India*	Asia *UAE*	Africa *Kenya*	Asia *Singapore*

Layout of the units

Each book is divided into ten units composed of three lessons. In the opening units pupils are introduced to key themes such as water, weather, settlement and the environment at increasing levels of complexity. The following units focus on places from around the UK, Europe and other continents. The overall aim is to provide a balanced coverage of geography.

Unit title
Identifies the focus of the unit and suggests links and connections to other subjects.

Lesson title
Identifies the theme of the lesson. The supporting copymaster also uses this title which makes it easy to identify.

Enquiry question
Suggests opportunities for open-ended investigations and practical activities.

Key word panel
Highlights key geographical words and terms which will be used during the lesson.

Introductory text
Introduces the topic in a graded text of around 100 words.

Discussion panel
Consists of three questions designed to draw pupils into the topic and to stimulate discussion. The first question often involves simple comprehension, the second question involves reasoning and the third question introduces a human element which helps to relate the topic to the child's own experience.

Graphics
Graphical devices ranging from maps to satellite images amplify the topic.

Data Bank
Provides extra information to engage children and encourage them to find out more for themselves.

Mapwork exercise
Indicates how the lesson can be developed through atlas and mapwork.

Investigation panel
Suggests a practical activity which will help pupils consolidate their understanding.

Summary panel
Indicates the knowledge and understanding covered in the unit.

Copymasters
Each lesson has a supporting copymaster which can be found in pages 30-59 of this book.

Layout of the units

Enquiry question

Lesson title

Unit title

Discussion panel

Graphic

Data Bank

Unit 1 Restless Earth

Lesson 1: Earthquakes and volcanoes

What do we know about the Earth's crust?

The ground beneath our feet seems firm and solid, yet every so often earthquakes and volcanoes make it shake and crack. Earthquakes and volcanoes happen suddenly, other Earth movements happen very gradually. Sometimes fossil sea shells are found in the rocks in high mountains. This proves to scientists that these rocks were once on the seabed.

▼ Earthquakes are measured by a seismograph. The graph shows how much the Earth moved during an earthquake on a Pacific island.

Discussion

What clues show that some mountains are made of rocks that were once under the sea?

What are the three sections that make up the Earth?

Why might volcanoes be found in lines or groups?

▼ The layers of rock on these cliffs were twisted and bent when the land was pushed up out of the sea by Earth movements.

Key words

crust	mantle
earthquake	seismograph
fossil	volcano

2

crust
core
mantle

▲ Earthquakes happen when two parts of the crust move apart or grind together. This photograph shows the San Andreas fault in California, USA, which stretches for hundreds of kilometres.

▲ When a volcano erupts, hot rocks and gases are forced to the surface. If the lava continues to flow for hundreds of years, high mountains, like Mount Ngauruhoe in New Zealand, can be built up.

Unit 1 • Restless Earth

Data Bank
- Between 50 and 70 volcanoes erupt each year – about one a week.
- Three-quarters of the world's volcanoes are in the 'ring of fire' around the Pacific Ocean.
- More than half the energy used in Iceland comes from hot rocks under the ground.

The Earth is made up of three different sections. The surface, or crust, is between six and 40 kilometres thick. It consists of solid rock. Beneath the crust is a section called the mantle. Parts of the mantle are so hot that the rocks have melted and flow like a sticky liquid. The core of the Earth is an even hotter ball of iron and nickel.

Mapwork
Working from an atlas or the internet, name six famous volcanoes. Add information about the date when they erupted and the country where they are found.

Investigation
Make up a diagram to show hot rocks coming to the surface in a volcano.

3

Key word panel

Investigation panel

Introductory text

Mapwork exercise

Lesson planning

Collins Primary Geography has been designed to support both whole school and individual lesson planning. As you devise your schemes and work out lesson plans you may find it helpful to ask the following questions. For example, have you:

- Given children a range of entry points which will engage their enthusiasm and capture their imagination?
- Used a range of teaching strategies which cater for pupils who learn in different ways?
- Thought about using games as a teaching device?
- Explored the ways that stories or personal accounts might be integrated with the topic?
- Considered the opportunities for practical activities and fieldwork enquiries?
- Encouraged pupils to use globes and maps where appropriate?
- Considered whether to include a global dimension?
- Checked to see whether you are challenging rather than reinforcing stereotypes?
- Checked on links to suitable websites, particularly with respect to research?
- Made use of ICT to record findings or analyse information?

- Made links to other subjects where there is a natural overlap?
- Promoted geography alongside literacy skills especially in talking and writing?
- Taken advantage of the opportunities for presentations and class displays?
- Ensured that the pupils are developing geographical skills and meaningful subject knowledge?
- Clarified the knowledge, skills and concepts that will underpin the unit?
- Identified appropriate learning outcomes or given pupils the opportunity to identify their own ones?

These questions are offered as prompts which may help you to generate stimulating and lively lessons. There is clear evidence that when geography is fun and pupils enjoy what they are doing it can lead to lasting learning. Striking a balance between light-hearted delivery and serious intent is part of the craft of being a teacher.

Misconceptions

There is a growing body of research which helps practitioners to understand more about how children learn primary geography and the barriers and challenges that they commonly encounter. The way that young children assume that the physical environment was created by people was first highlighted by Jean Piaget. The importance and significance of early childhood misconceptions was further illuminated by Howard Gardner. More recent research has considered how children develop their understanding of maps and places. Children's ideas about other countries and their attitudes to other nationalities form another very important line of enquiry. Some key readings are listed in the references on page 15.

Lesson summary

The table below provides an overview of the lessons in *Collins Primary Geography Pupil Book 6*. Individual schools may want to adapt the lessons and associated activities according to their particular needs and circumstances.

Theme	Unit	Lesson 1	Lesson 2	Lesson 3
Planet Earth	Restless Earth	Earthquakes and volcanoes	Creating landscapes	Rocks and soils in the UK
Water	Drinking water	Water, water, everywhere	Water supplies	Conserving water
Weather	Local weather	The right conditions	Micro-climates	Influencing the weather
Settlements	Planning issues	Reasons for development	Old sites, new uses	Planning game
Work and travel	Transport	Travelling further, travelling faster	Transport problems	Hidden costs
Environment	Conservation	Threatened wildlife	Antarctica	Conservation projects
United Kingdom	England	Learning about England	Finding out about Sandwich	Living in Sandwich
Europe	Europe	Introducing Europe	The European Union	Celebrating Europe
North and South America	South America	Learning about the Amazon	Using the rainforest	Saving the Amazon
Asia and Africa	Asia	South East Asia	Investigating Singapore	A Singapore family

Studying the local area

The local area is the immediate vicinity around the school and the home. It consists of three different components: the school building, the school grounds, and local streets and buildings. By studying their local area, children will learn about the different features which make their environment distinctive and how it attains a specific character. When they are familiar with their own area, they will then be able to make meaningful comparisons with more distant places.

There are many opportunities to support the lessons outlined in *Collins Primary Geography* with practical local area work. First-hand experience is fundamental to good practice in geography teaching, is a clear requirement in the programme of study and has been highlighted in guidance to Ofsted inspectors. The local area can be used not only to develop ideas from human geography but also to illustrate physical and environmental themes. The checklist below illustrates some of the features which could be identified and studied.

Physical geography	Human geography
Hill, valley, cliff, mountain, rock, slope, soil, wood	Origins of settlements, land use and economic activity
River, stream, pond, lake, estuary, coast	House, cottage, terrace, flat, housing estate
Slopes, rock, soil, plants and other small-scale features	Roads, stations, harbours
Local weather and site conditions	Shops, factories and offices
	Fire, police, ambulance, health services
	Library, museum, park, leisure centre

All work in the local area involves collecting and analysing information. An important way in which this can be achieved is through the use of maps and plans. Other techniques include annotated drawings, bar charts, tables and reports. There will also be opportunities for the children to make presentations in class and perhaps to the rest of the school in assemblies

Studying places in the UK and wider world

Collins Primary Geography Pupil Book 6 contains studies of the following places in the UK and wider world. Place studies focus on small scale environments and everyday life. By considering people and describing their surroundings, the information is presented at a scale and in a manner which relates particularly well to children. Research shows that pupils tend to reach a peak of friendliness towards other countries and nations at about the age of ten. It is important to capitalise on this educationally and to challenge prejudices and stereotypes.

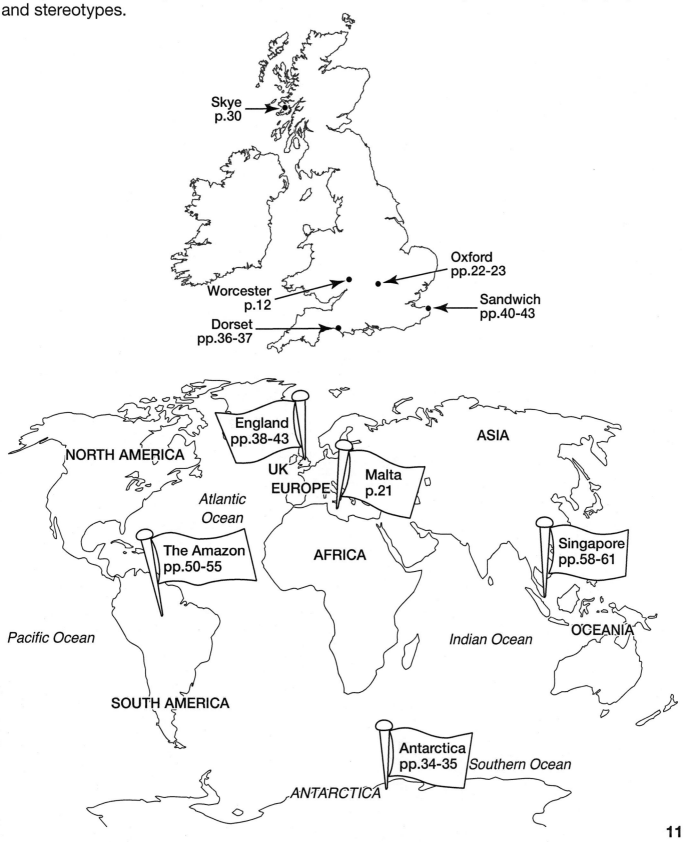

Differentiation and progression

Collins Primary Geography sets out to provide access to the curriculum for children of all abilities. It is structured so that children can respond to and use the material in a variety of ways. Within each unit there is a range of exercises and discussion questions. This means activities can be selected which are appropriate to individual circumstances.

Differentiation by outcome
Each lesson starts with an introductory text and linked discussion questions which are designed to capture the children's imagination and draw them into the topic. There are opportunities for slower learners to relate the material to their own experience. More able children will be able to consider the underlying geographical concepts. The pace and range of the discussion can be controlled to suit the needs of the class or group.

Differentiation by process
Children of all abilities benefit from exploring their environment and conducting their own investigations. The investigation activities include many suggestions for direct experience and first-hand learning. Work in the local area can overcome the problems of written communication by focusing on concrete events. There are also opportunities for taking photographs and conducting surveys as well as for making lists, diagrams and written descriptions.

Differentiation by task
The mapwork and investigation exercises can be modified according to the pupils' ability levels. Teachers may decide to complete some of the tasks as class exercises or help slower learners by working through the first part of an exercise with them. Classroom assistants could also use the lessons with individual children or small groups. More able children could be given extension tasks. Ideas and suggestions for extending each lesson are provided in the information on individual units (pages 16-25).

Progression
The themes, language and complexity of the material have been graded to provide progression between each title. However, the gradient between different books is deliberately shallow. This makes it possible for the books to be used interchangeably by different year groups or within mixed ability classes. The way that this might work can be illustrated by considering a sample unit. For instance, in Book 3 the unit on weather introduces children to hot and cold places around the world. Book 4 looks at ways of recording the weather, Book 5 focuses on the seasons and Book 6 considers local weather conditions. This approach provides opportunities for reinforcement and revisiting which will be particularly helpful for the less able child.

Assessment

Assessment is often seen as having two very different dimensions. Formative assessment is an on-going process which provides both pupils and teachers with information about the progress they are making in a piece of work. Summative assessment occurs at defined points in a child's learning and seeks to establish what they have learnt and how they are performing in relation both to their peers and to nationally agreed standards. *Collins Primary Geography* provides opportunities for both formative and summative assessment.

Formative assessment

- The discussion questions invite pupils to discuss a topic, relate it to their previous experience and consider any issues which may arise, thereby yielding information about their current knowledge and understanding.
- The mapwork exercises focus especially on developing spatial awareness and skills and will indicate the pupils' current level of ability
- The investigation activities give pupils the chance to extend their knowledge in ways that match their current abilities.

Summative assessment

- The panels at the end of each unit highlight key learning outcomes. These can be tested directly through individually designed exercises.
- The copymasters (see pages 30-59) can be used to provide additional evidence of pupil achievement. Whether used formatively or summatively they are intended to broaden and consolidate understanding.

Reporting to parents

Collins Primary Geography is structured around geographical skills, themes and place studies which become more complex from one book to another. As children work through the units they can build up a folder of work. This will include mapwork and investigations in the local area and will provide evidence of breadth, progression and achievement in geography. It will also be a useful resource when teachers report to parents about whether an individual child is above average, satisfactory, or in need of help in geography.

National curriculum reporting

There is a single attainment target for geography and other National Curriculum subjects. This simply states that

'By the end of each key stage, pupils are expected to know, apply and understand the matters, skills and processes specified in the relevant programme of study.'

This means that assessment need not be an onerous burden and that evidence of pupils' achievement can be built up over an entire Key Stage. The assessment process can also inform lesson planning. Establishing what pupils have demonstrably understood helps to highlight more clearly what they still need to learn.

High quality geography

The regular reviews of geography teaching in the UK undertaken by Ofsted provide a clear guidance.

Ofsted recommendations
Ofsted recommends schools to:
- focus on developing pupils' core knowledge and sense of place.
- ensure that geography elements are clearly identified within topic based work.
- maximize opportunities for fieldwork in order to improve pupil motivation.
- make the most of new technology to enthuse pupils and provide immediacy and relevance.
- provide more opportunities for writing at length and focused reading.
- enable pupils to recognise their responsibilities as citizens.
- develop networks to share good practice.
- provide subject specific support and professional development opportunities for teachers.

Primary Geography Quality Mark
The Primary Geography Quality Mark set up by the UK Geographical Association is another measure of excellence. This provides a self-assessment framework designed to help subject leaders. There are three categories of award. The 'bronze' level recognises that lively and enjoyable geography is happening in your school, the 'silver' level recognises excellence across the school and the 'gold' level recognises excellence that is shared and embedded in the community beyond the school. The framework is divided into four separate cells (a) pupil progress and achievement (b) quality of teaching (c) behaviour and relationships (d) leadership and management. For further details see www.geography.org.uk.

Achieving accreditation for geography in school is a useful way of badging achievements and identifying targets for future improvement. The Geographical Association provides a wide range of support to help teachers with this process. In addition to an ambassador scheme and Continuing Professional Development (CPD) sessions it produces a journal for primary schools, *Primary Geography*, three time a year. Other key sources are the Geographical Association website, the *Primary Geography Handbook* and books and guides for classroom use such as *Geography Plus*.

Finding time for geography
The pressures on the school timetable and the demands of the core subjects make it hard to secure adequate time for primary geography. However, finding ways of integrating geography with mathematics and literacy can be a creative way of increasing opportunities. Geography also has a natural place in a wide range of socia studies and current affairs whether local or global. It can be developed through class assemblies and extra-curricular studies. Those who are committed to thinking geographically find a surprising number of ways of developing the subject whatever the accountability regime in which they operate.

Ofsted inspections

Ofsted inspections are designed to monitor standards of teaching in schools in England and Wales. Curriculum development is an on-going process and inspectors do not always expect to see totally completed programmes. What they are looking for is evidence of carefully planned strategies which are having a positive impact on the quality of teaching. However, inspectors must also note weaknesses and highlight aspects which need attention. If curriculum development is already in hand in your school, it should receive positive support. The following checklist provides prompts which may help prepare for inspections.

1 Identify a teacher who is responsible for developing the geography curriculum.
2 Provide a regular opportunity for discussing geography teaching in staff meetings.
3 See that all members of staff are familiar with the geography curriculum.
4 Decide how geography will fit into your whole school plan.
5 Make an audit of current geography teaching resources to identify gaps and weaknesses.
6 Discuss and develop a geography policy which includes statements on overall aims, topic planning, teaching methods, resources, assessment and recording.
7 Discuss the policy with the governors.
8 Devise an action plan for geography which includes an annual review procedure.

References and further reading

Bonnett, A. (2009) *What is Geography?* London: Sage
Butt, G. (Ed.) (2011) *Geography, Education and the Future,* London: Continuum
Catling, S. and Willy, T. (2009) *Teaching Primary Geography,* Exeter: Learning Matters
DfE (2013) National Curriculum in England: Programmes of study – Key Stages 1 and 2 available at www.education.gov.uk/schools/teachingandlearning/curriculum/primary
Lucas, B. and Claxton, G. (2011) *New Kinds of Smart,* Maidenhead: Open University Press
Martin, F. (2006) *Teaching Geography in Primary Schools : Learning to live in the world,* Cambridge: Kington
Ofsted (2011) *Geography: Learning to Make a World of Difference,* London: Ofsted
Scoffham, S. (Ed.) (2010) *Primary Geography Handbook,* Sheffield: Geographical Association
Scoffham, S. (Ed.) (2013) *Teaching Geography Creatively,* London: Routledge
Wiegand, P. (2006) *Learning and Teaching with Maps,* London: Routledge

The Geographical Association

The Geographical Association (GA) provides extensive support and advice for teachers including a range of excellent publications such as the *Everyday Geography* and *Geography Plus* series. As well as holding an annual conference, the GA also produces a journal for primary practitioners, *Primary Geography,* which is published three times a year. To find out more and learn about the latest developments in geography education visit the website at www.geography.org.uk.

Information on the units

Unit 1: RESTLESS EARTH

Earth tremors can happen almost anywhere in the world, including the UK. However most tremors occur within well-defined earthquake belts as the different plates which make up the Earth's crust move around. The vibrations are recorded on a machine called a seismograph and the amount of energy released is described using the Richter scale.

Lesson 1: EARTHQUAKES AND VOLCANOES
What do we know about the Earth's crust?

This lesson introduces the idea that the Earth's crust, whilst it may appear solid, is actually constantly moving as it is carried around by convection currents in the mantle. Earth tremors, whether from earthquakes or volcanoes, are common occurrences. As they discuss different earth movements some pupils may start talking about tectonic plates. These are not considered in this lesson due to the complexities involved.

Mapwork *Finding out the names and locations of a few famous volcanoes will naturally lead pupils to want to find out more.*

Investigation *There are many different types of volcano with different shapes and structure. The classic example is a cone made from layers of ash and lava.*

Lesson 2: CREATING LANDSCAPES
What forces shape the land?

Rocks are worn away very slowly over long periods of time. Even adults find it difficult to understand how small changes can eventually reduce mountain ranges to sea level. It is enough at this stage simply to introduce pupils to the general idea.

Investigation *The survey of wear and tear in the school grounds is suggested as a way of introducing pupils to the idea of erosion in a meaningful way.*

Lesson 3: ROCKS AND SOILS IN THE UK
How has the landscape of the UK formed?

There are plenty of clues in the landscape which reveal its geological history. In the mountains of Wales, Scotland and the Lake District, for example, the U-shaped valleys and sharp ridges indicate that the land has been shaped by glaciers. Elsewhere fossils in the rocks provide clues about conditions millions of years ago. The UK is unusual in having a particularly varied geology with rocks from nearly all periods of geological history. The oldest rocks in the UK date back to around 600 million years ago. It is by working from a variety of sources that geologists have been able to put rocks into chronological order.

Mapwork *Many of us don't ever think about the rocks that our under our feet, in our buildings or in the manufactured goods that we use on a daily basis. Pupils will not need to go far when they devise their trails.*

Investigation *Children often enjoy contributing items they have collected to a display table. In addition to a variety of colours and textures, fossils will give a rock collection added interest.*

Rocks in the street

Thinking about how rocks are used as building materials provides natural links to the study of materials and their properties in science.

Copymasters *See 1 ,2 and 3 for linked extension exercises.*

Unit 2: DRINKING WATER

Water, like food, is a basic human need. Each person needs a minimum of about 50 litres of water a day to sustain a reasonable quality of life. Water consumption varies enormously between countries and indeed different communities. Around the world only about five per cent of water is used for domestic purposes. Industry takes 20 per cent and the rest is used for irrigation. However demand for water is rising along with higher living standards and population growth. As a result shortages are becoming increasingly common, especially in arid areas.

Lesson 1: WATER, WATER, EVERYWHERE

Is there enough water in the world?

In recent years there has been increasing interest in water security as people have come to recognise that fresh water is a finite resource. Part of the problem is that supplies are irregular. Periods of drought and water scarcity can alternate with floods and heavy rain. Finding ways to store surpluses is one way of increasing protection against variations in weather and climate.

Mapwork *This exercise introduces the idea of catchment areas. It also suggests one way of defining a region and highlights links which might not otherwise be apparent.*

Investigation *Pupils may find it hard to visualize the data presented in the tap diagram. It will help them to relate to the figures if you fill a litre bottle with water as a demonstration.*

Lesson 2: WATER SUPPLIES

Why is clean water so important?

Polluted water carries disease. In England it was responsible for serious outbreaks of cholera in the nineteenth century. Today it is estimated that 80 per cent of the diseases in developing countries are related to dirty water and poor sanitation.

Mapwork *The diagrams of water supply will show the route the water takes and are thus a form of map*

Investigation *This exercise touches on the sensitive issue of disparities between the developed and developing world. As pupils learn about global inequalities it is important to avoid promoting negative stereotypes. The case studies and units on different regions around the world have been designed with this in mind.*

Lesson 3: CONSERVING WATER

Are we using water wisely?

The main idea in this unit is that water can be used again and again.

Investigation *The idea of making 'wise decisions' is an important one for environmentalists. It acknowledges that people have a legitimate claim to water resources but encourages restraint.*

A water survey

The survey illustrates how water can be conserved. You could develop the work by asking the children to write a report on ways of saving water in your school.

Mapwork As they devise their flow diagrams pupils might consider where the water in their homes comes from and what happens to it after it goes down the plug hole.

Copymasters *See 4, 5 and 6 for linked extension exercises.*

Unit 3: LOCAL WEATHER

As well as studying general weather patterns, geographers are also interested in how the weather can vary from place to place. Local differences include frost pockets in valleys, sea breezes near the coast and heat islands in towns. On a larger scale, mountain ranges force air to rise and shed moisture, creating a rain shadow on the leeward side. They also funnel currents of air to create local winds. People who live and work in the countryside have learnt to exploit these forces and use them to their advantage. Although new technology has greatly increased our power over the environment, the best new developments still take account of local circumstances rather than ignoring them.

Lesson 1: THE RIGHT CONDITIONS
Why do people want to control the weather?

You might want to consider the advantages and disadvantages of controlling our immediate environment. It extends the range of conditions in which people can live and work but the energy costs are often high, particularly if the associated environmental damage is taken into account.

Mapwork *The mapwork relates this theme to the child's immediate environment.*

Investigation *The idea of a survival capsule taps into pupil's imagination but can be brought back to everyday life by looking at houses and homes around the world.*

Lesson 2: MICRO-CLIMATES
How does the weather vary between places?

The main objective in this lesson is to show how people, plants and animals respond to the local environment. This reinforces the idea of habitats which is developed further in the study of Dorset heaths on page 36.

Investigation *You might develop the travel brochure idea by devising a spoof advertisement showing adverse weather in different locations rather than wall to wall sunshine which is the norm.*

Lesson 3: INFLUENCING THE WEATHER
How are people affecting the weather?

In the nineteenth and twentieth centuries London and other UK cities suffered from smog which claimed many lives. Air pollution is now less visible but perhaps even more pernicious. As you explore this theme with pupils stress solutions as well as problems. It is important that they are not left feeling powerless.

Finding the right site

There will be a surprising range of micro-climates even on a small site. These variations will be most apparent on a sunny day. Clues such as moss and lichen are tell-tale signs of damp and shady environments and even the hardiest plants struggle to survive on windy corners.

Mapwork *It will help if you have a large scale plan of your school for pupils to work from.*

Investigation *The good news story brings a positive dimension to this lesson and suggests to children that there are solutions as well as problems.*

Copymasters *See 7, 8 and 9 for linked extension activities.*

Unit 4: PLANNING ISSUES

As the pressure on land has increased in the UK, it has become necessary to introduce more and more planning laws. Until the early years of last century, people could build houses and factories almost anywhere they wanted. The first legislation was mainly concerned with controlling disease. Gradually, local authorities have been given powers to control how land is used. Since 1947, all new development needs to have planning permission. National parks, and urban and rural conservation areas have also been designated. Children are introduced to urban planning issues in this unit. Case studies of Oxford and Malta illustrate how controls can influence the way that settlements develop. The children are asked to consider the qualities of their school site and how it might be used.

Lesson 1: REASONS FOR DEVELOPMENT
Why are there conflicts over land use?
The diagram on page 20 is a visual representation of some of the different ways that people compete to use the same space. Reconciling different interests is a complicated process. Once land is used for development it rarely returns to a natural state. Local Plans provide a framework and general presumptions which help steer decision making.
Investigation *Looking at old maps can be a fascinating activity – much will depend on the documents you are able to track down.*
Living on an island
With a population of over 1000 people per square kilometre, Malta is one of the most densely populated countries in Europe. The case study emphasises the idea that land is a finite resource and that people have to live within their means.
Mapwork *As they look at each grid square pupils will have to decide on the main use and ignore other activities.*

Lesson 2: OLD SITES, NEW USES
How can old sites be redeveloped?
The redevelopment of the car factory site at Cowley illustrates how needs change over time and how public consultation is part of the planning process. It also shows how new developments do not always have to be put on greenfield sites. Redeveloping so-called 'brownfield' sites is one way of conserving land.
Mapwork *You might want to put pupils into groups so they can share ideas about what they would like to see in a new school building.*

Investigation *The key point in this investigation is that there were a number of different options at Cowley and that choices had to made between them.*

Lesson 3: PLANNING GAME
How are planning decisions made?
Simulations and role plays can lead be a particularly effective way of engaging children and are thus a feature of good practice in primary geography education. The planning game which is outlined here might be developed further by involving outsider advisers such as an architect, builder or planner to act as consultant to advise pupils on their proposals.
Mapwork *As well as developing pupils map reading skills, this exercise highlights the different features and facilities in an urban area. Albert Square will be familiar to many children as the setting for the TV soap opera 'Eastenders'.*
Investigation *Encourage pupils to think 'geographically' as they make their advertisements by using appropriate language and including maps and plans.*

Copymasters *See 10, 11 and 12 for linked extension exercises.*

Unit 5: TRANSPORT

There has been a phenomenal growth of the speed and availability of travel over the last century. In the 1920s, for example, it took the best part of a week to travel from Britain to the USA by boat. Now this same journey can be completed in a matter of hours. Mass air travel has allowed people to move round the world as never before. Holiday resorts in places as far apart as Thailand and Mexico attract visitors from Europe and North America. At the same time the growth of trade and international finance has linked different economies together as never before. Globalisation has changed the way that people live their lives and made them increasingly interdependent.

Lesson 1: TRAVELLING FURTHER, TRAVELLING FASTER
What are the opportunities for travel in the world today?
This first lesson introduces pupils to international and global transport networks. The drawbacks and benefits of mass travel provide a subsidiary theme.
Mapwork *In identifying places where three or more routes converge pupils will be considering accessibility. You might want to discuss whether the most accessible points are necessarily the most desirable for people and business.*
Investigation *Once they have made up a word search for European cities children could make up searches on other themes as a homework or extension activity.*

Lesson 2: TRANSPORT PROBLEMS
Can roads cope with more traffic?
Coping with traffic has been a major challenge for many decades. Building motorways and bypasses was once seen as a way of solving traffic problems but it is now recognized that new roads also attract traffic and create problems in other places. Similar difficulties affect air travel as the air routes around London are now operating at nearly full capacity.
Investigation *The photograph of the lorry highlights the tension between our desire for cheap goods and mass transport and the impact of vehicles on the environment.*

Keeping traffic moving
The flow diagram highlights how traffic management involves a combination of strategies rather than individual initiatives.
Mapwork *In addition to recording physical objects such as bollards and fences, pupils may want to annotate their plans to record parking regulations and other rules.*

Lesson 3: HIDDEN COSTS
How do vehicles affect people and the environment?
You might give this lesson a positive slant by getting pupils to think of solutions rather than dwelling on the problems which vehicles cause. The road bridge to Skye opened in 1995 and was used by over 600 000 vehicles in its first year of operation. Protesters who complained were particularly concerned about the damage to the environment, loss of wildlife, fumes from the traffic and the cost of the scheme. They also argued that the tolls were too high and that the historic ferry would be put out of business.
Finding out about local transport
Investigation *You may need to adapt the questionnaire to match your local circumstances. Extend the work by asking the children to make a map of safe routes to school. They could also write a short report about any changes they would like to see.*

Copymasters *See 13, 14 and 15 for linked extension exercises.*

Unit 6: CONSERVATION

The battle to save endangered species has a long history. Fifty years ago environmental groups launched campaigns to save individual animals, such as whales, tigers and rhinos. Although these campaigns achieved considerable success, it became clear that much more was needed to safeguard the survival of other, less glamorous life forms. For this reason, in the 1980s, attention switched to preserving whole environments, such as rainforests, ancient woodlands and coral reefs. Whole habitats and ecosystems have the advantage of containing a balance of life within them. The problem is that people will only choose to preserve these environments if they also bring social and economic benefits. This has led to the notion of sustainable development in which people try to use the environment without upsetting its ecological balance. Making wise choices which enable us to live within the carry capacity of the planet is now seen as a key challenge for the twenty-first century. Many people believe the stakes are getting steadily higher.

Lesson 1: THREATENED WILDLIFE
Why are many plants and animals endangered?

This lesson introduces the topic of environment and sustainability by focusing on flagship species.

Mapwork *Get the children to find out about endangered creatures in different parts of the world including the UK and Europe. It is important to establish that conservation is a global challenge and doesn't just apply to the rainforest and other distant places.*

Investigation *See that pupils access child friendly sites when they do their research – many conservation groups have areas for children.*

Lesson 2: ANTARCTICA
Why should Antarctica be conserved?

Antarctica is a unique and beautiful continent which has been protected from development due to its harsh climate and isolated position. Its future as a pristine environment depends on international co-operation. The mixture of ecological, social and political issues which surround its protection make for a particularly interesting case study.

Antarctica world park

The arguments for and against a world park are considered in this second part of the lesson.

Investigation *Although Amundsen's expedition was the first to reach the South Pole, Captain Scott's story is much more well-known in the UK*

Lesson 3: CONSERVATION PROJECTS
What are people doing to conserve the environment?

This case study about the Dorset heathlands shows how easily environments can be destroyed by piecemeal development. However it also shows how concerted action can not only reverse decline but lead to lasting improvements.

Mapwork *There are sites within walking distance of most schools which have wildlife potential and the opportunities for links with science makes this an attractive fieldwork activity.*

How can we keep a balanced environment?

Many children will have seen organic food in the shops. Understanding how organic food is produced will enhance their ideas and understanding.

Investigation *Exploring the advantages and disadvantages of organic farming will give children the opportunity to begin to formulate their own views and to take ownership of their learning.*

Copymasters *See 16, 17 and 18 for linked extension activities.*

Unit 7: ENGLAND

England is the largest country in the United Kingdom. It is about the same size as Scotland, Wales and Northern Ireland put together, but has four times the population. London is the biggest city with over seven million inhabitants. It is a worldwide centre for banking and commerce and Heathrow airport is the busiest airport in Europe. Despite the changes of the last few decades, England is still highly industrialised. Steel, chemicals, textiles, aircraft, cars, engineering, machinery and electronics are some of the main industries. There are considerable regional differences, particularly between the old industrial areas of the north and the south where finance and banking dominate.

Lesson 1: LEARNING ABOUT ENGLAND
What is England like?
There is a balance of physical and human geography in this lesson. The aim is to provide an brief overview of England which pupils can build on as their knowledge extends.
Mapwork *Children might sort the cities in other ways e.g. alphabetically or in order of size.*
Investigation *The images might focus on different themes such as buildings, coastlines or heritage sites.*

Lesson 2: FINDING OUT ABOUT SANDWICH
How has Sandwich developed?
Sandwich is an ancient town which has preserved many medieval and historic features. Once an important port, it fell into decline as the river which linked it to sea silted up. Refugees from the Low Countries settled in Sandwich in large numbers in the seventeenth century. In the eighteenth century the first market gardens in England were set up in the area following the Dutch example.
Mapwork *A guided walk or trail is a way to explore a locality and it will provide a context for pupils to develop their mapwork and other related geographical skills.*
Investigation *If you find it difficult to access information relating to your immediate area, pupils could devise a timeline for their region and focus on a number of different places.*

Lesson 3: LIVING IN SANDWICH
New developments
The location of Sandwich close to the mainland of Europe has always influenced its development. The Energy Park is linked to France which is just 30 km away. The redevelopment of the chemical factory offers a wide range of jobs and helped to rejuvenate the town.
Quality of life
People have different views about the changes which are happening in and around Sandwich. These are explored in the speech bubble comments.
Investigation *This activity encourages pupils to think about local changes and possible future developments. This can be a difficult concept for children who tend to think that places have always been the same.*

Copymasters *See 19, 20 and 21 for linked extension activities.*

Unit 8: EUROPE

Europe is one of the smallest but also one of the most varied continents. It stretches from Portugal and Ireland in the west to the Ural Mountains in the east. The coastline is deeply indented and rich in natural harbours. Seas, like the Mediterranean, Adriatic and Aegean, have served as the focus for many ancient civilisations. From the sixteenth to the twentieth centuries Europe dominated world affairs as it spearheaded the Industrial Revolution. Today, although eclipsed by the USA and China, it still retains a key position in terms of industry, agriculture, trade and finance. Europe is also helping to forge new approaches to environmental thinking as people grapple with the problems of living within the finite carrying capacity of the planet.

Lesson 1: INTRODUCING EUROPE
What are the regions of Europe?
This lesson uses a map to introduce the physical landscape of Europe. The portraits of the three children illustrate regional differences.
Mapwork *No country is completely covered by forest but Sweden and Finland would both have large forest areas.*
Investigation *Pupils might identify a number of different routes between the two cities. You might extend the exercise by tracing routes between other cities such as London and Istanbul, which, whilst they are not marked on the map are easy to locate.*

Lesson 2: THE EUROPEAN UNION
How can countries work together?
Although some people have doubts about the way the European Union works, it is an interesting example of international co-operation. Many social, environmental and economic problems require international rather than national solutions. One of the challenges of the current time is to find forms of government which are capable of responding at both a local and global level.
The European Union in action
Mapwork *Once pupils have made their list from an atlas they could check their answers by downloading a list from the internet.*
Investigation *You could extend this exercise by thinking of reasons for not joining the EU as a prelude to a class debate on the pros and cons.*

Lesson 3: CELEBRATING EUROPE
What is special about Europe?
You could use the information on pages 48 and 49 as the basis for your own class celebration. In doing this you will have to decide whether you want to keep a strong geography focus or whether to adopt an interdisciplinary approach.
Mapwork *It will help the children if their maps are in colour. You may have some old maps which are no longer needed which pupils can use. Colour photocopies or colour maps from the internet offer viable alternatives.*
Investigation *See that pupils are clear in their own minds about the answers to their questions and encourage them to frame the questions as unambiguously as possible. This work offers clear links to literacy.*

Copymasters *See 22, 23 and 24 for linked extension activities*

Unit 9: SOUTH AMERICA

Rainforests extend approximately ten degrees north and south of the Equator. Although they only cover a relatively small proportion of the Earth's surface, they contain well over half of all plant and animal species. Most of these have never been studied or named by scientists. Amazonia is the most important and largest remaining rainforest region in the world. It is the ancestral home to around a million native Indians. Although Indians many have moved to cities, there are still thought to be some forest groups that have had never been in contact with the outside world.

Lesson 1: LEARNING ABOUT THE AMAZON

What is the Amazon like?

Many pupils will have heard of the Amazon but they may not be aware of where it is in the world – UK children know relatively little about South America.

Why is the rainforest being cleared?

For countries like Brazil, Amazonia is a frontier zone waiting to be exploited and developed. It is rich in mineral resources, has huge potential for hydroelectric power and can provide space for landless peasants. The wood from the forests also earns valuable export income.

Mapwork *This activity contextualizes the Amazon and sets it in an international context.*

Investigation *Pupils could include charts, diagrams and other visual information in their fact files.*

Lesson 2: USING THE RAINFOREST

What is it like to live in the rainforest?

The case study on page 52 outlines a traditional way of living which uses the forest in a sustainable manner. This contrasts with the destructive uses described in the previous lesson.

Why is the rainforest so important?

Questions about the pros and cons of clearing the rainforest lie behind the information on this page and might lead to an in-depth class project, if time is available.

Investigation *This activity considers the immediate and local effects of forest clearance. However, the rainforest also helps to regulate world climate. If more than around 50 per cent of it is cleared it is believed that it could trigger changes in the climate which will affect both remaining forest areas and planetary systems.*

Lesson 3: SAVING THE AMAZON

What was Chico Mendes trying to do?

The speed at which the rainforest is being cleared has alarmed people around the world. Chico Mendes and the Rubber Tapper's Union pioneered ways of exploiting the wealth of the forest in a sustainable way. This idea has considerable potential as it recognises the economic value of the natural environment.

Mapwork *It will be hard for children to make informed decisions about the best places for new reserves but the principle of saving some areas and sacrificing others is well worth exploring.*

Investigation *Pupils could illustrate their timelines using drawings in the panels.*

Copymasters *See 25, 26 and 27 for linked extension exercises.*

Information on the units

Unit 10: ASIA

Southeast Asia is a geographical region which lies wholly within the tropics. With the mainland of Asia to the north west and the Pacific Ocean to the east, SE Asia occupies a strategically important location. Air and shipping routes are focused on Singapore and the Malay peninsula. The coastal areas are studded with islands. Indonesia and the Philippines are both on tectonic plate boundaries and the scene of considerable volcanic activity. Since 1967 the countries of SE Asia have been linked together economically and politically through ASEAN (the Association of South East Asian Nations). Rapid industrialization and export-led growth has led to some of these countries being described as tiger economies.

Lesson 1: SOUTHEAST ASIA
What is Southeast Asia like?

This lesson introduces themes from both physical and human geography. A key feature is the rapid development which has occurred over the last 50 years. Pupils need to appreciate that although SE Asia was historically part of European empires it now exhibits many of the features of a modern industrialised world.

Mapwork *The largest cities include Singapore, Jakarta, Bangkok, Manila, Kuala Lumpur, Yangoon and Ho Chi Minh City.*

Investigation *Remember that the fact files can include graphical as well as numerical information.*

Lesson 2: INVESTIGATING SINGAPORE
What is Singapore like?

The growth and development of Singapore in many ways symbolizes the growth and development which characterizes many parts of SE Asia. Founded as a trading post less than 200 years ago the swampy and unhealthy islands at the tip of the Malay peninsula have now become a thriving modern nation. Chinese, Malayan and Indian communities have all contributed to Singapore's success. Trade links with the rest of the world and the associated banking and finance industries are crucial to its continuing prosperity.

Mapwork *The fact that Singapore lies almost exactly on the Equator is a natural opportunity to find out about other cities with a similar latitude.*

Investigation *Pupils might want to stress the advantages of Singapore's location on the sea routes from Europe to China and Japan and its proximity to Australia in their advertisements.*

For a case study of what attracts a modern business to Singapore find out why Rolls Royce has decided to invest in its Seletar facility.

Lesson 3: A SINGAPORE FAMILY
What is it like to live in Singapore?

The case study of a Singapore family traces how one family has responded to the economic forces which underlie the development of the city.

Planning for the future

The shortage of land in Singapore means that there is a premium on using all resources as wisely as possible. New buildings and water are two key examples of how careful planning can bring long term benefits.

Mapwork *Get the pupils to cut out cardboard to represent the blocks of flats so they can test out alternative positions as they devise their plans.*

Investigation *You might include this activity as part of a topic on water using the lessons in Unit 2.*

Copymasters *See 28, 29 and 30 for linked extension exercises.*

Copymaster matrix

Unit	Copymaster	Description
Restless Earth	1 Earthquakes and volcanoes	Pupils colour a cross section diagram of the Earth and distinguish different layers.
	2 Creating landscapes	Children complete a crossword and say how different forces shape the land.
	3 Rocks and soils in the UK	Pupils children compare different UK landscapes using information in the book.
Drinking water	4 Water, water everywhere	Children devise a block graph to show how much water is consumed in different activities.
	5 Water supplies	The children complete a world map to show the places where people do not have clean water.
	6 Conserving water	The children make drawings and describe three different ways of saving water
Local weather	7 The right conditions	A practical exercise in which the children find out how their school deals with rain, cold, light and ventilation.
	8 Micro-climates	The children compare different habitats in an Alpine valley using pictures and descriptions.
	9 Influencing the weather	Children make a list of different local air pollution problems and consider how they might be solved
Planning issues	10 Reasons for development	Pupils complete a table listing the advantages of different types of development.
	11 Old sites, new uses	Pupils devise land use symbols and give brief reasons for using vacant sites in different ways.
	12 Planning game	The children compile an estate agent's brochure for their school site.
Transport	13 Travelling further, travelling faster	A survey in which children compare the advantages and disadvantages of air travel.
	14 Transport problems	A snakes and ladders game to show how road improvement schemes create as many problems as they solve.
	15 Hidden costs	A survey sheet which the children can use to find out about local traffic problems.

Aim	Teaching point
To consolidate pupils' understanding of what lies beneath the Earth's surface.	See that pupils have an understanding of the scale of the diagram – it is 6000 km to the centre of the Earth.
To reinforce understanding of different processes of erosion.	The children will need to read the text carefully before writing down their ideas.
To show that the landscapes of the UK were formed in different ways.	Extend the work by finding the different landscapes in other parts of the UK.
To illustrate the range of ways that we use water in our daily lives.	Activities such as brushing teeth and drinking will only show up on the graph as a vertical line.
To highlight how access to clean water is still a world-wide problem.	Discuss the problems caused by dirty water and possible solutions.
To draw attention to ways of solving water supply problems.	Make sure that the children understand why different solutions are needed in different places.
To illustrate how buildings are designed to create a comfortable environment.	Allow the children to collect examples from around the school rather than restricting them to the classroom.
To illustrate how local site conditions can influence the weather.	The children could find out changes in vegetation on Kilimanjaro as an extension activity.
To alert pupils to the problems of air pollution and their impact on health.	This activity could be completed as a group or class exercise to allow pupils to pool their ideas.
To emphasise how empty sites can be developed in a variety of ways.	See pupils understand how different categories overlap. For example, farming could be good for the environment and housing developments have implications for transport.
To show that planning often involves balancing different interests and considerations.	Discuss how each site might be used before the children make their choices.
To help children see the limitations and potential of redevelopment.	It will be useful for the children to have access to a plan of the school.
To alert pupils to the way that all innovation has a hidden cost.	It will be interesting to see the results of the survey and perhaps extend the work as a class debate.
To show that traffic problems cannot be solved simply by road improvement.	The snakes and ladders boards will last longer if they are mounted on card.
To promote local fieldwork and investigations.	You will need to select a suitable place to conduct the survey. The children should work in groups.

Copymaster matrix

Unit	Copymaster	Description
Conservation	16 Threatened wildlife	Pupils make notes and drawings to complete a chart of endangered wildlife
	17 Antarctica	An exercise in which children speculate on changes in Antarctica over the past two centuries.
	18 Conservation projects	The children complete a picture of a heathland habitat and describe its special features.
England	19 Learning about England	Working from the maps in the pupil book, children collect information about specified grid squares.
	20 Finding out about Sandwich	The children make drawings of some of the key features of Sandwich.
	21 Living in Sandwich	Pupils select terms from a word bank to describe six different scenes then write a short report.
Europe	22 Introducing Europe	Pupils complete a key and colour five key Western European countries on an outline map.
	23 The European Union	A mapwork exercise showing how the European Union expanded between 1957 and 1995 and the present day.
	24 Celebrating Europe	A game in which pupils collect four cards relating to a European country
South America	25 Learning about the Amazon	Using an outline world map pupils identify rainforest, desert and polar regions.
	26 Using the rainforest	Pupils colour an outline rainforest drawing and consider the impact of forest clearance.
	27 Saving the Amazon	Pupils devise a speech to represent the views of either Chico Mendes or Da Silva.
Asia	28 Southeast Asia	A mapwork game in which pupils identify different countries in Southeast Asia.
	29 Investigating Singapore	Pupils compile a set of data about Singapore using different given headings.
	30 A Singapore family	Pupils construct a simple trapezium model illustrating futures thinking.

Aim	Teaching point
To identify flagship species that are threatened or in serious decline.	Pupils will need to research their own examples in order to complete the activity sheet.
To raise awareness of the unique but fragile Antarctic environment.	Discuss what changes might have happened before pupils start this exercise.
To highlight the ecological value of a heathland habitat.	You could create a class display following the format of the sheet.
To consolidate understanding of four figure grid references using a UK map.	Remind the children to start at the bottom left hand comer going 'along the corridor and up the stairs'.
To show how drawings words and maps can be combined to create a place portrait.	The children could devise a similar picture map of their own area.
To the features which contribute to the quality of an environment.	Pupils could use their own words to supplement the terms in the word bank.
To gain familiarity with the political map of Western Europe.	Suggest that pupils could select a single colour for those countries which are not named on the map.
To show how the European Union has grown increasingly larger.	The children will need atlases in order to identify the different countries.
To consolidate geographical knowledge in an enjoyable way.	Invite pupils to devise their own European countries game as an extension activity.
To contextualise Amazonia alongside other key biomes.	Invite children to name the different regions shown on the map.
To highlight the value of the rainforest environment.	There a number of creatures which are 'hidden' in the drawing. Further work into rainforest animals would be a natural extension activity.
To show that there are two sides to the debate about the future of the rainforest.	Use this activity as preparation for a role play or class assembly about the rainforest.
To consolidate children's understanding of southeast Asia.	Singapore occupies such a small territory that it cannot be represented on the map.
To build a portrait of Singapore that draws on physical, human and environmental geography.	Talk with the children about the range of information they might include under each heading.
To explore some of the ways in which Singapore is thinking ahead and building resilience.	The models could form part of a larger display on sustainability and futures thinking.

1 Earthquakes and volcanoes

Name ....

1. Colour the empty boxes in the key.

2. Use these colours to complete the diagram.

3. Write a sentence about each word.

Key	
sea	blue
land	green
crust	brown
mantle	orange
core	yellow

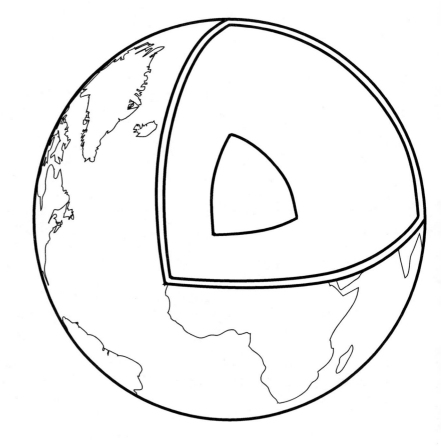

The Earth's crust _____

_____

The mantle _____

_____

The core _____

_____

2 Creating landscapes

Name ....

1. Use the clues to help you complete the crossword.

Across

① A current of air

② Large streams

③ A ridge of water found in seas and oceans

Down

① A force that breaks rock apart

② Frozen water

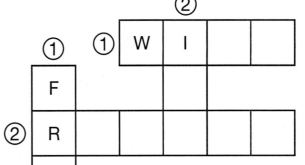

2. How does each force shape the landscape?

Force	Effect on landscape
Frost	
Rivers	
Waves	
Wind	
Ice	

1. Colour the drawings of the different landscapes from around the United Kingdom.

2. Explain how each landscape was formed.

Landscape	How was it formed?
Snowdonia 	
Herefordshire	
Yorkshire	
Oxfordshire	

4 Water, water everywhere   *Name* ....

1. Add up the numbers by the water drops to find out how much water one
   person might use in a day.

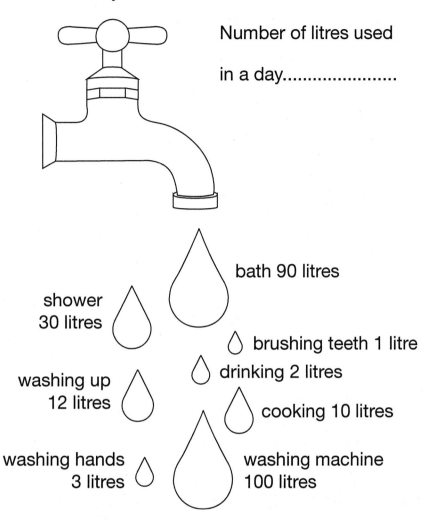

Number of litres used

in a day.....................

bath 90 litres

shower
30 litres

brushing teeth 1 litre

drinking 2 litres

washing up
12 litres

cooking 10 litres

washing hands
3 litres

washing machine
100 litres

2. Make a bar chart of the amount of water used for each activity.

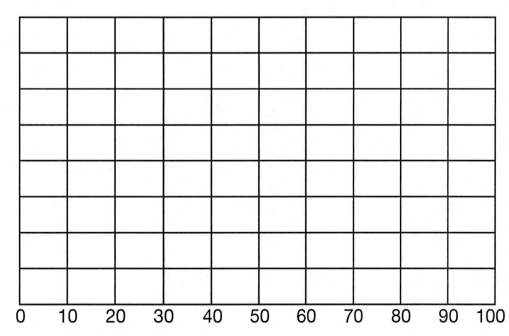

brushing teeth

drinking

washing hands

cooking

washing up

shower

bath

washing machine

0   10   20   30   40   50   60   70   80   90   100

⑤ Water supplies

1. Colour the world map to show the places where many people do not have clean water. Colour the key.

2. Write down some of the problems caused by dirty water.

Key: Places with poor water supply ☐   Other places ☐

Problems caused by dirty water

6 Conserving water

1. Make drawings of three ways of saving water.

2. Write a few words saying how each one does this.

	How does it save water?
	....
	How does it save water? ....
	How does it save water? ....

7 The right conditions

Name ....

1. Draw pictures and write descriptions of how your school deals with each of these weather problems.

Rain	How are the rooms kept dry?
	....
Cold	How are the rooms kept warm?
	....
Light	How are the rooms kept light?
	....
Ventilation	How does fresh air circulate?
	....

8 Micro-climates

Name ....

1. Colour the pictures of the plants and mountain valley.

2. Draw a line from each plant to the place where it grows.

3. Write a sentence about the weather conditions at each site.

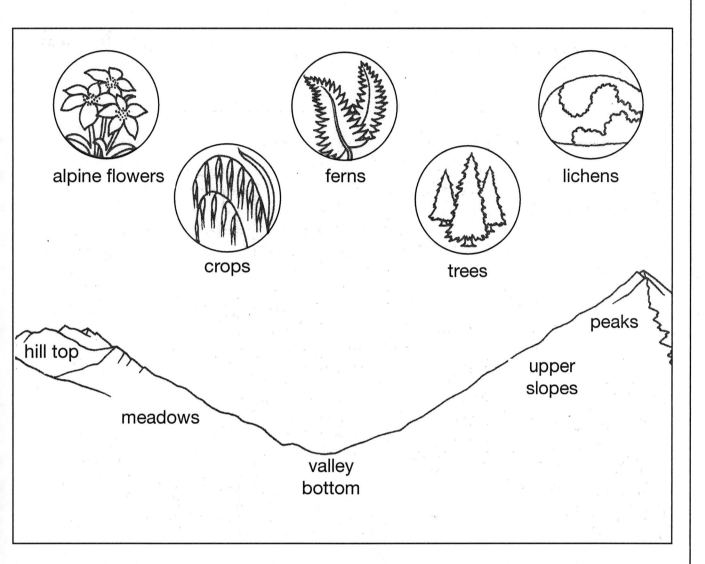

alpine flowers

crops

ferns

trees

lichens

hill top

peaks

upper slopes

meadows

valley bottom

Site	Weather conditions
Hill top	
Meadows	
Valley bottom	
Upper slopes	
Peaks	

1. Make a list of ten pollution problems in the area round your school.

2. Decide how long you think each will last and colour the correct box to show your answer.

Pollution problem	How long will it last?		
	under 1 year	1–10 years	over 10 years
1.			
2.			
3.			
4.			
5.			
6.			
7.			
8.			
9.			
10.			

3. Say how one of the problems could be solved.

....

....

....

....

10 Reasons for development

1. Colour the drawing.

2. Write a sentence about the advantage of each possible use.

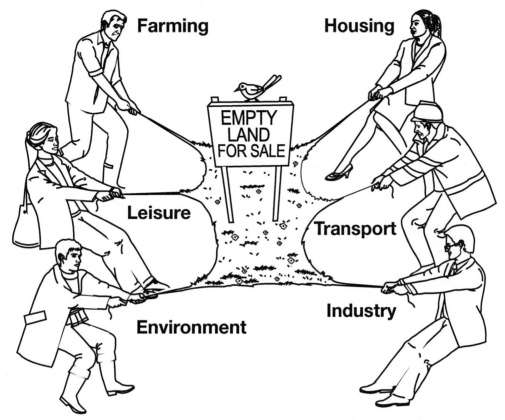

Possible use	Advantage
Farming	....
Housing	....
Leisure	....
Transport	....
Environment	....
Industry	....

⓫ Old sites, new uses

Name ....

1. Draw symbols showing different ways of using land.

housing	industry	farming	leisure	environment

2. What is the best way of using each site on the plan below?

3. Draw symbols on the plan and write a sentence in the table giving your reason.

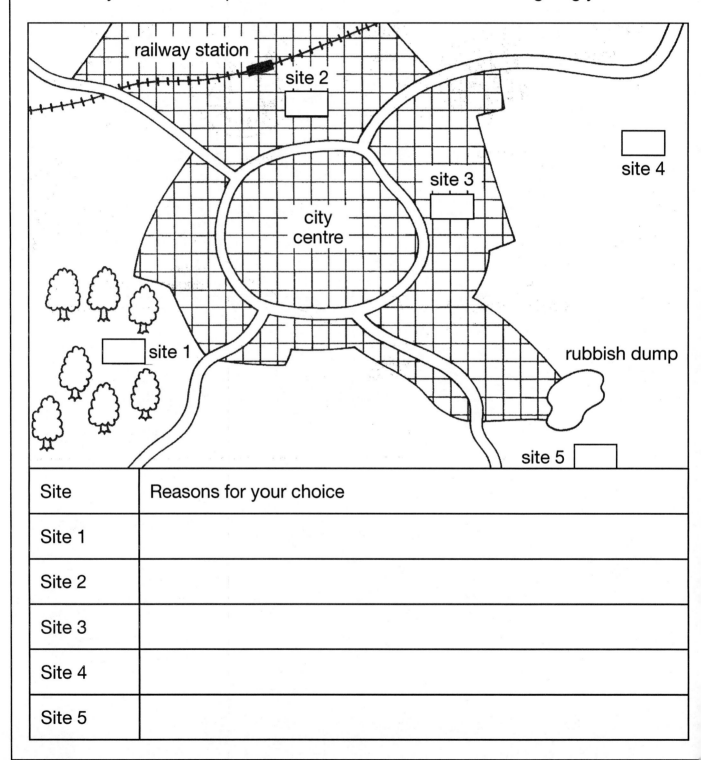

Site	Reasons for your choice
Site 1	
Site 2	
Site 3	
Site 4	
Site 5	

⑫ Planning game

1. Write down the information you would put in a sale brochure for your school.

SCHOOL FOR SALE
Visits by appointment only

Name of school ....

Number of rooms ....

Open spaces/grounds ....

Any special facilities ....

....

Possible uses ....

....

How can the site be reached by car or public transport?

....

....

....

....

....

Plan of the school

13 Travelling further, travelling faster

Name ....

1. Complete the drawings and descriptions in the table below.

2. Circle one of the scores in each row.

ADVANTAGES	DESCRIPTION	PLUS SCORE	
	Flying is the safest way to travel.	OK	+ 1
		good	+ 2
		excellent	+ 3
	Flying is very fast.	OK	+ 1
		good	+ 2
		excellent	+ 3
		OK	+ 1
		good	+ 2
		excellent	+ 3
DISADVANTAGES	DESCRIPTION	MINUS SCORE	
	No good for heavy and bulky goods.	annoying	+ 1
		bad	+ 2
		serious	+ 3
		annoying	+ 1
		bad	+ 2
		serious	+ 3
	Planes are very noisy.	annoying	+ 1
		bad	+ 2
		serious	+ 3

3. Add up your plus and minus scores.   + [   ]   − [   ]

4. Which total is larger? What does this show you about your view of flying?

....

....

14 Transport problems

Name ....

1. Colour the snakes and ladders game below.

2. Play the game with a partner. You will need a dice and a couple of counters.

FINISH	55	Better roads create more traffic.	53	52	Shortage of oil and petrol.	50
43	44	45	Traffic noise causes stress.	47	48	49
42	41	40	39	38	37	Park and ride scheme.
29	30	31	32	33	34	Fumes cause health problems.
Bypass built around villages.	27	26	25	24	23	22
15	16	17	Motorways link large cities.	19	20	21
14	13	12	11	Increase in road accidents.	9	8
START	New traffic schemes improve traffic flow.	3	Ring road around city centres.	5	6	7

15 Hidden costs

Make a survey of the traffic problems in your area.

1. Ask passers-by which traffic problem they think is most serious.

2. Colour a square to show their answer.

3. Write a few sentences about what you have discovered from the survey.

Traffic Problem	1	2	3	4	5	6	7	8	9	10	11	12
Noise from traffic												
Not enough crossing places												
Traffic travelling too fast												
Roads without pavements												
Not enough safety barriers												
Too many parked cars												
Shortage of cycle routes												
Exhaust fumes												
Heavy lorries												
Rush hour traffic jams												

....

....

....

....

....

Name ....

1. Colour the drawings of threatened creatures.

2. Say why each one is threatened.

3. Add three more examples of your own.

Whales	Eagles	Butterflies
....	....	....

Orchids	Rhinos	Teak trees
....	....	....

....	....	....

17 Issues in Antartica

1. Draw what the penguins might have seen 200 years ago.

2. Draw what they might be looking at today.

3. Label your drawings using green for natural features and red for things brought in by people.

1. Draw the heathland animals in the empty circles.

2. Write a report saying what makes the heathland special, how it was nearly destroyed and the way it was saved.

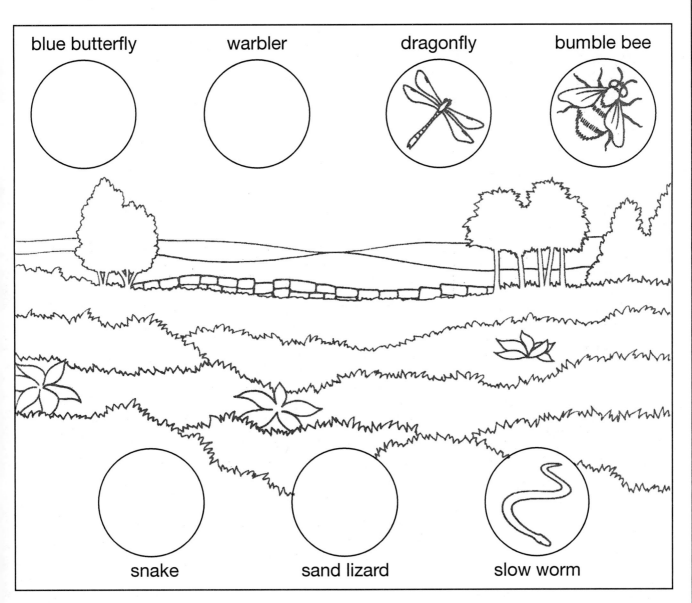

blue butterfly   warbler   dragonfly   bumble bee

snake   sand lizard   slow worm

Report

....

....

....

....

....

....

1. Look at each grid square. For each square listed, name one of the features shown on either of the maps on pages 38-39.

2. Mark these features on the map.

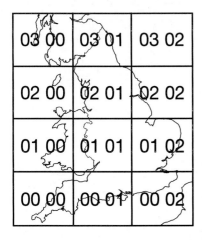

Square 00 00
Square 00 01
Square 00 02
Square 01 00
Square 01 01
Square 01 02
Square 02 01
Square 02 02

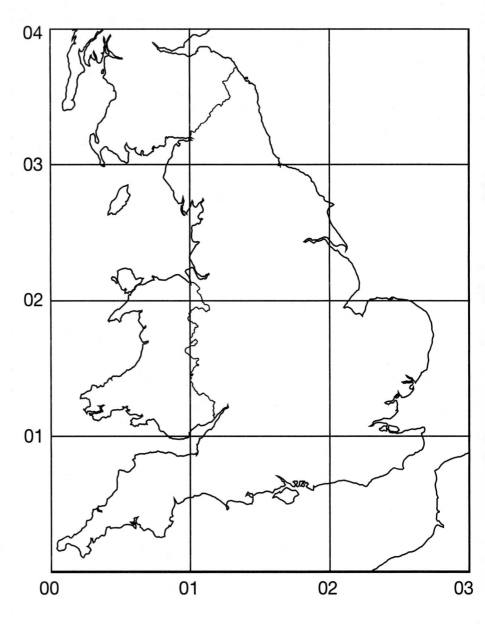

Name ....

1. Colour the river, roads and old town centre on the map.

2. Make drawings of the different features in the boxes.

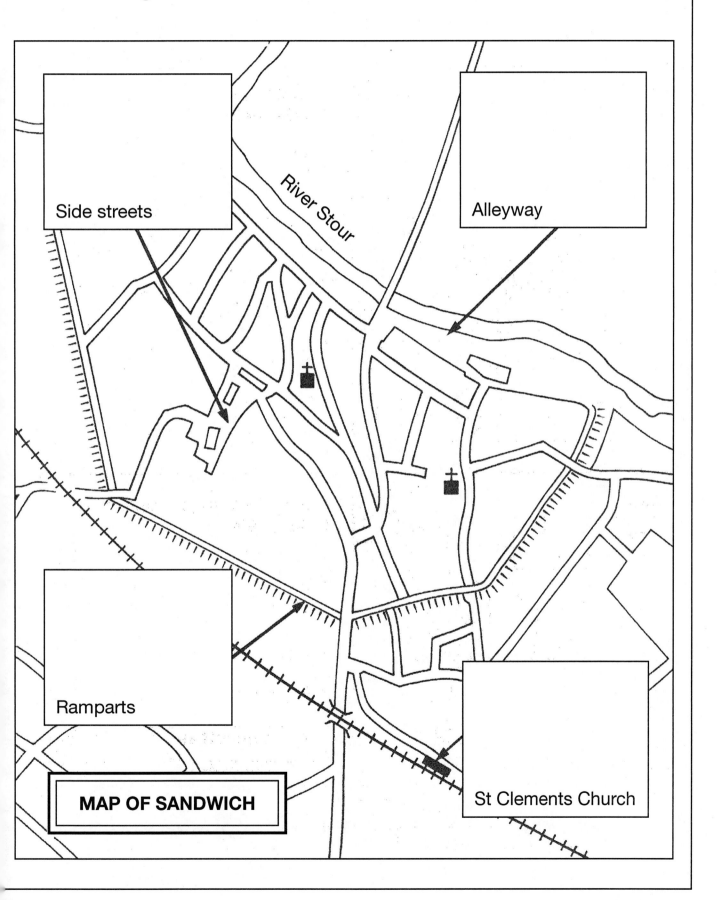

Side streets

River Stour

Alleyway

Ramparts

St Clements Church

MAP OF SANDWICH

21 Living in Sandwich

1. Write one of the words from this list under each picture.

noisy   beautiful   dull   smoky   interesting

smelly   peaceful   ugly   quiet   convenient

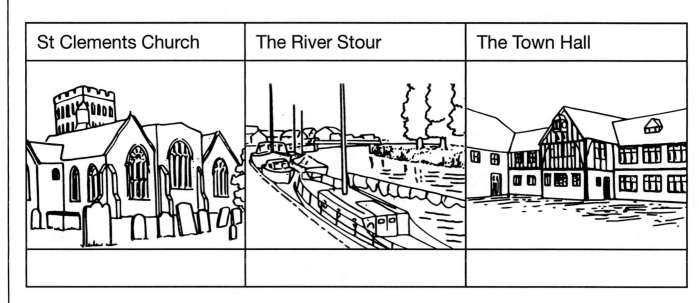

St Clements Church	The River Stour	The Town Hall

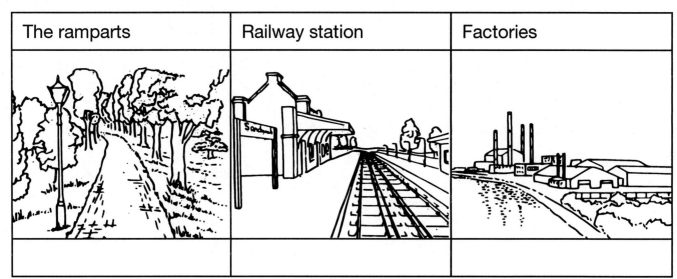

The ramparts	Railway station	Factories

2. Write a short report about living in Sandwich.

....

....

....

....

....

Name ....

1. Colour the code boxes in the key.
2. Colour the countries on the map.
3. Name the capital cities.

Country	Code	Capital
UK	red	
France	green	
Spain	orange	
Germany	yellow	
Italy	brown	

23 The European Union

1. List the countries which belonged to the EU in 1957 and 1995.

2. Colour the maps.

3. How many countries belong to the EU today? ....

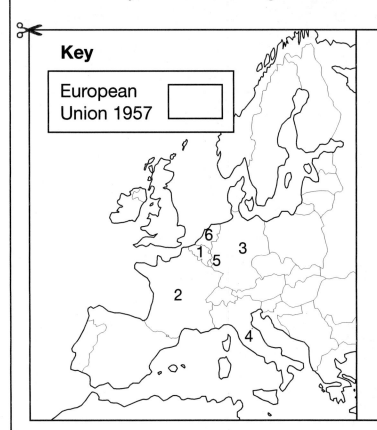

Key

European
Union 1957 [ ]

Countries in the European
Union, 1957

1 ....

2 ....

3 ....

4 ....

5 ....

6 ....

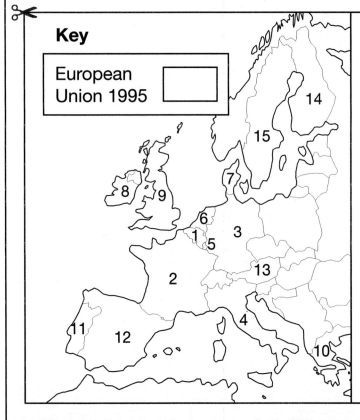

Key

European
Union 1995 [ ]

Countries in the European Union,
1995

1	9	
2	10	
3	11	
4	12	
5	13	
6	14	
7	15	
8		

Play the countries game in groups of three.

1. Colour the cards, cut them out and put them face down on the table.

2. Each player has to say which country set they want to collect.

3. Take turns to pick up a card, put it back if it is not in your set.

4. The winner is the first to collect a complete country set.

Germany	France	Italy
black red yellow	blue white red	green white red
Brandenburg Gate, Berlin	Eiffel Tower, Paris	Colosseum, Rome
Guten Tag	Bonjour	Buon giorno

25 Learning about the Amazon

Name ....

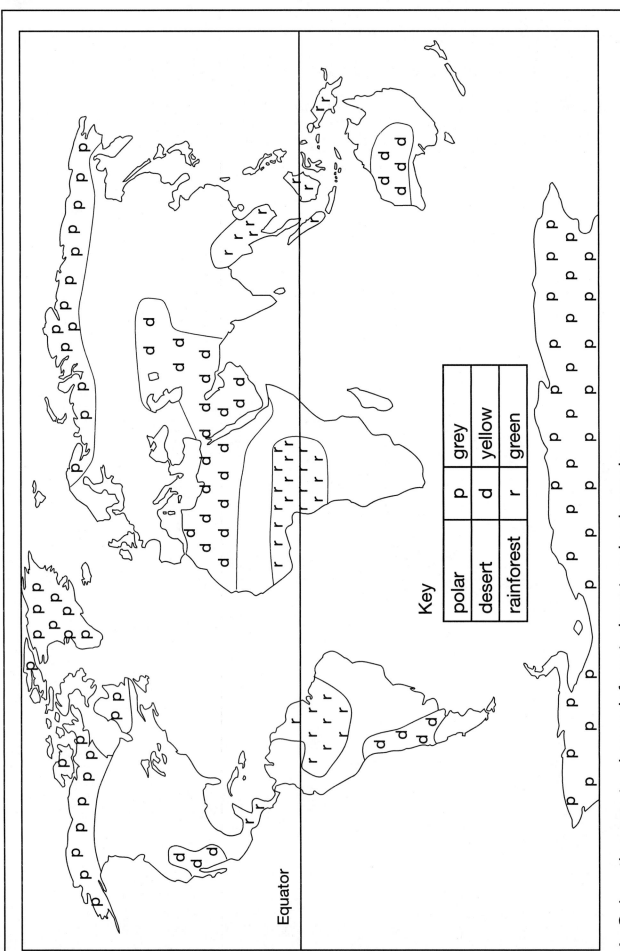

Equator

Key

polar	p	grey
desert	d	yellow
rainforest	r	green

1. Colour the map to show rainforest, desert and polar regions.

2. What two things does this tell you about the Amazon (a) .... (b) ....

Using the rainforest

1. Colour the rainforest picture.

2. What would happen if the trees were cut down? Write a few sentences in the space under the picture.

....

....

....

Hold a debate about changes in the rainforest.

1. Ask the teacher if you are Chico Mendes or Da Silva.

2. Colour your person.

3. Make a list of the things you want to say in your speech.

4. Design a slogan for the banner.

Chico Mendes
Rubber tapper

Da Silva
Landowner

Ideas for my speech

....

....

....

....

....

....

....

....

....

....

Banner

1. Colour the map of Southeast Asia.

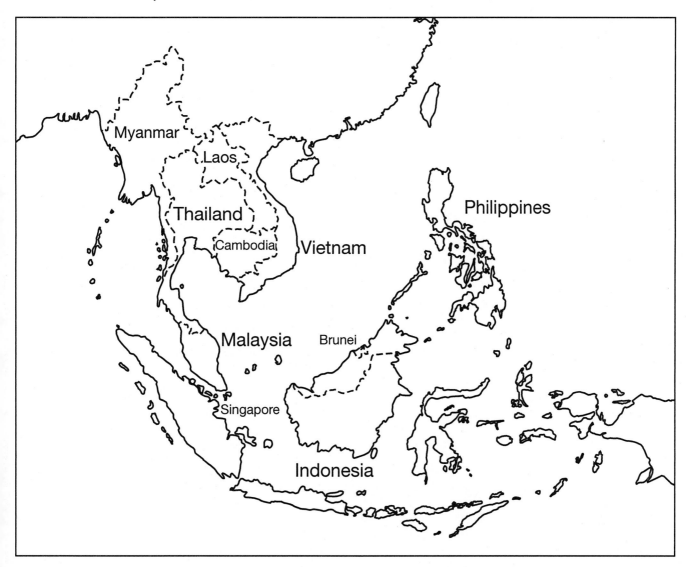

2. Play a game with a partner. Take turns to throw a pair of dice. The winner is the person to land on all of the countries.

Country	Tick each time you land	Country	Tick each time you land
1 Myanmar		7 Malaysia	
2 Thailand		8 Singapore	
3 Vietnam		9 Brunei	
4 Cambodia		10 Indonesia	
5 Laos		11 Philippines	
6 *Miss a turn*		12 *Miss a turn*	

1. Make up a data and information sheet about Singapore.

Map	History

Climate	Communication

Trade and industry	Environment

Name ....

Water supply

Tampins new town

Planning for the future

Flap

1. Make notes and drawings under each of the headings on the diagram.
2. Cut round the edge, fold along the dotted lines and glue down the flap to make a model.

Geography in the English National Curriculum

A new primary geography curriculum was introduced in England in 2014. This new curriculum provides a framework for schools to follow but leaves teachers considerable scope to select and organise the content according to their individual needs. It should also be noted that the curriculum is only intended to occupy a proportion of the school day and that schools are free to devise their own studies in the time that remains.

Purpose of study

The aim of geographical education is clearly articulated in the opening section of the Programme of Study which states:

A high quality geography education should inspire in pupils a curiosity and fascination about the world and its people that will remain with them for the rest of their lives. Teaching should equip pupils with knowledge about diverse places, people, resources and natural and human environments, together with a deep understanding of the Earth's key physical and human processes. As pupils progress, their growing knowledge about the world should help them to deepen their understanding of the interaction between physical and human processes, and of the formation and use of landscapes and environments. Geographical knowledge, understanding and skills provide the frameworks and approaches that explain how the Earth's features at different scales are shaped and interconnected and change over time.

Subject content

The National Curriculum provides the following general guidance for each Key Stage:

Key Stage 1

Pupils should develop knowledge about the world, the United Kingdom and their locality. They should understand basic subject-specific vocabulary relating to human and physical geography and begin to use geographical skills, including first-hand observation, to enhance their locational awareness.

Key Stage 2

Pupils should extend their knowledge and understanding beyond the local area to include the United Kingdom and Europe, North and South America. This will include the location and characteristics of a range of the world's most significant human and physical features. They should develop their use of geographical knowledge, understanding and skills to enhance their locational and place knowledge.

Teachers who are familiar with the previous version of the curriculum will note the increasing emphasis on factual and place knowledge. For example, there is a greater focus on learning about the UK and Europe. Map reading and communication skills are also highlighted. On the other hand, there are no specific references to the developing world and sustainability is not mentioned directly. However, there is an expectation that schools will work from the Programmes of Study to develop a broad and balanced curriculum which meets the needs of learners in their locality. This provides schools with scope to enrich the curriculum and rectify any omissions which they may perceive.

Key Stage 2 Programme of study

The elements specified in the Key Stage 2 programme of study are listed below. The summary provided here should read alongside the statements about the wider aims of the curriculum. There is no suggestion that pupils should work to individual statements.

Focus
Extend knowledge of UK, Europe and North and South America
Location of world's most significant human and physical features
Knowledge, understanding and skills to enhance locational and place knowledge
Locational knowledge
Locate the world's countries
Use maps to focus on countries, cities and regions in Europe
Use maps to focus on countries, cities and regions in North America
Use maps to focus on countries, cities and regions in South America
Name and locate counties of the UK
Name and locate cities of the UK
Geographical regions of the UK
Topographical features of the UK
Changing land use patterns of the UK
Significance of latitude and longitude
Significance of Equator, Northern and Southern Hemisphere, Tropics of Cancer/Capricorn, Arctic/Antarctic circles, Prime Meridian
Time zones
Day and night
Place knowledge
Regional study within UK
Regional study in a European country
Regional study in North America
Regional study in South America
Human and physical geography
Climate zones
Biomes and vegetation belts
Rivers and mountains
Volcanoes and earthquakes
Water cycle
Types of settlement and land use
Economic activity including trade links
Distribution of natural resources including energy, food, minerals, water
Skills and fieldwork
Use maps, atlases, globes and digital mapping
Use eight points of the compass
Use four and six figure grid references
Use symbols and keys (including OS maps)
Fieldwork skills

WORLD MAP

WORLD COUNTRIES

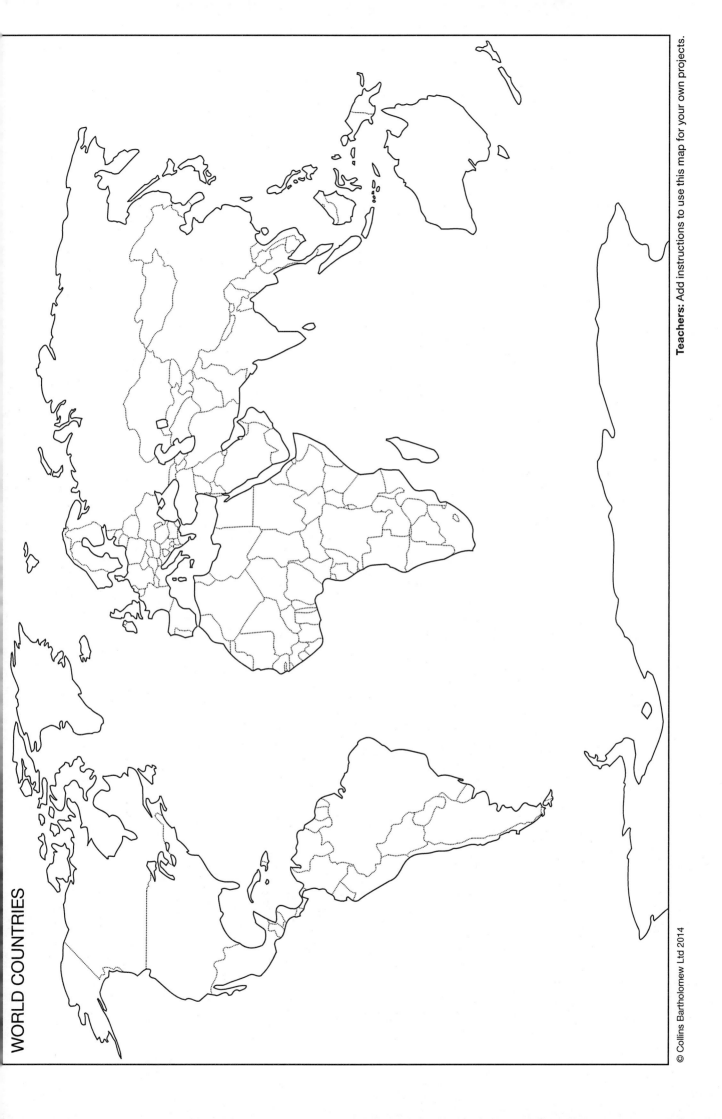

Primary Geography Teacher's Book 6
Collins
An imprint of HarperCollins Publishers
Westerhill Road
Bishopbriggs
Glasgow
G64 2QT

ISBN 978-0-00-756367-8

Imp 001

British Library Cataloguing in Publication Data
A catalogue record for this book is available from the British Library.

Printed by RR Donnelley at Glasgow, UK.

Acknowledgements

Additional original input by Terry Jewson

Cover designs Steve Evans illustration and design

Illustrations by Jouve Pvt Ltd p40

Photo credits:

All images from www.shutterstock.com